MORE CLEAN JOKES FOR KIDS

compiled by
Dan Harmon
with
Tamela Hancock Murray

BARBOUR
PUBLISHING, INC.
Uhrichsville, Ohio

© MCMXCIX by Barbour Publishing, Inc.

ISBN 1-57748-600-5

Published by Barbour Publishing, Inc., P.O. Box 719, Uhrichsville, Ohio 44683   http://www.barbourbooks.com

ᴇᴄᴘᴀ Member of the
Evangelical Christian
Publishers Association

Printed in the United States of America.

MORE CLEAN JOKES FOR KIDS

ANIMALS

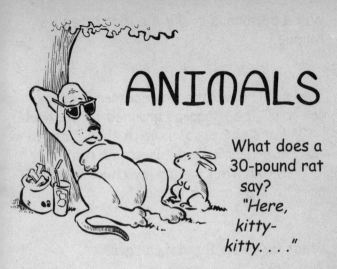

What does a 30-pound rat say?
"Here, kitty-kitty. . . ."

* * *

What did one skunk say to the other?
"Let us spray."

* * *

What's very large and heavy, has a gray trunk, lives in Scotland, and has baffled investigators for centuries?
The Loch Ness elephant.

Will a poisonous snake die if it bites its tongue?

✶ ✶ ✶

"Oh, no! The weather forecaster is calling for rain!" the kangaroo groaned to the rabbit.

"What's the problem with that?" asked the rabbit. "We could use some rain."

"Yes, but that means my children will have to stay inside to play."

✶ ✶ ✶

What do you call a dozen rats?
Scary.

✶ ✶ ✶

What do you call a snake who gets elected mayor?
A civil serpent.

✶ ✶ ✶

Why do kangaroos paint themselves green?
So they can hide in a bowl of spinach.

Why do porcupines never lose games?
Because they always have more points than any other animal.

✶ ✶ ✶

What did one fox say to another?
"I'm tired of being hounded all the time."

✶ ✶ ✶

What do you call mouse shoes?
Squeakers.

✶ ✶ ✶

What did the boy porcupine say after he kissed the girl porcupine?
Ouch!

✶ ✶ ✶

"Do you think the skunk would be considered a very popular animal?" the teacher asked.

"Not exactly—but it's always the scenter of attention," the student answered.

"That's a beautiful new wool sweater you're wearing!" marveled Tammy. "It's so thick and warm! I wonder how many sheep it took to make a sweater that size."

"I don't know," said Rhonda. "Actually, I didn't know sheep could do handiwork."

* * *

Why did the otter cross the road?
    To get to the otter side.

* * *

What do you call flying monkeys?
    Hot-air baboons.

* * *

What kind of infants prefer goat milk?
    Infant goats.

* * *

What do you call a rabbit with the sniffles?
    A runny bunny.

How do mice keep their breath fresh all day long?

They rinse with mousewash.

✳ ✳ ✳

What's huge and gray and goes around in circles?

A hippopotamus in a revolving door.

✳ ✳ ✳

How did the chimpanzee break out of its cage?

With a monkey wrench.

✳ ✳ ✳

What animal looks a lot like an aardvark?

Another aardvark.

✳ ✳ ✳

What goes 80 miles an hour underground?

A prairie dog on a motorcycle.

A pair of zebras were wandering in Africa when they heard the thunderous sound of hooves over the horizon. A massive herd of giraffes appeared, running their way in a blinding cloud of dust. The zebras took cover behind a tree and waited for the giraffes to pass. Then they continued wandering.

A few hours later, another large herd of giraffes approached, stirring up a storm of dust. Again, the zebras got out of the way.

Near sundown, they found themselves in the path of a third mob of giraffes. Standing behind a rock, coughing from the thick dust as the tall animals rushed past, one zebra turned to the other and said, "I think we should move away. There's too much giraffic around here to suit me."

✳ ✳ ✳

What's the happiest animal in the wild?
The happypotamus.

Santa Claus was confused when he found three red-nosed reindeer as he prepared his sleigh. "What's this?" he asked Mrs. Claus. "Which one is Rudolph?"

Mrs. Claus wiped the noses of the three reindeer with her apron. Amazingly, only one red-nosed reindeer—the true Rudolph—remained.

"It's no real mystery," she explained. "Dancer and Prancer have been eating my cherry cobbler again."

✮ ✮ ✮

Why does a giraffe have a long neck?
So it can't smell its feet.

✮ ✮ ✮

When is the best time for a dog to come in the house?
When the door is open.

Why is it hard to talk to a ram?

He keeps butting in.

★ ★ ★

How does an elephant get out of a small car?

The same way he got in.

★ ★ ★

TONGUE TWISTER

The skunk sat on the stump.
The stump said the skunk stunk.
The skunk said the stump stunk.
Who stunk?

ARITHMETIC

1+1=2

"If you have 10 pieces of bubble gum and you give away 4, what do you have then?" the teacher asked.

"I have 6 pieces of gum and 4 new friends!" the student figured.

* * *

Teacher: "Two trains are headed toward each other on the same track. They're both traveling 60 miles per hour, and they're 30 miles apart. How soon will they collide?"

Student: "Much too soon."

"My math teacher doesn't make sense," said Janet.

"Why do you think that?" asked Shayna.

"Yesterday she taught us that 9 plus 1 equals 10. Today she claims 7 plus 3 equals 10."

✳ ✳ ✳

Teacher: "Richie, if I offered you a choice between a basket with 36 bananas and a basket with 63 bananas, which would you choose?"

Richie: "The basket with 36 bananas."

Teacher: "Now Richie, surely you know 63 is more than 36."

Richie: "Yes, ma'am. That's why I'd pick the first basket. I can't stand bananas."

✳ ✳ ✳

Where do math teachers prefer to operate?
On multiplication tables.

"Mom, how far away is the moon?" the little boy asked.

"About 240,000 miles."

"How far away is the ocean?"

"Well, the nearest one to us is the Pacific Ocean. That's about 500 miles from here, as the crow flies."

"Is the moon as big as the Pacific Ocean?"

"I'm not sure. The moon is roughly 2,000 miles in diameter, and the Pacific Ocean is about that far across, at the widest part. So I suppose in a way, you might say they're sort of the same size."

The little boy thought about that for a while, then asked one more question. "Well, how far away is Phoenix?"

"By car, Phoenix is about 120 miles from us."

The boy shook his head. "I don't get it at all. The moon is a quarter of a million miles away, and I can see the moon clearly at night. But I can't see Phoenix, 120 miles from here. I can't even see the Pacific Ocean."

AUTOMOBILES

"This car
has never been
involved in a wreck," assured the
auto salesman.

"It *is* a wreck," said the wise customer.

★ ★ ★

"Why are you wearing your winter coat?"

"I'm waxing my car."

"Why do you need a winter coat to wax a car?"

"The wax container says a heavy coat makes the shine last longer."

"Dad, why don't we park our car on the street?"

"Because we have a driveway. The car's safer there. That's what driveways are for."

"If it's for parking cars, then why do we call it a driveway?"

∗ ∗ ∗

What did the driver say when she came to a fork in the road?

"This must be the place to eat."

∗ ∗ ∗

What kind of rabbits are good at fixing flat tires?

Jackrabbits.

∗ ∗ ∗

"How did your dog get that nasty lump on it's head?" asked Sam.

"It was chasing a parked car," said Tom.

"My dad rides to work in a carpool."

  "What does that mean?"

  "I'm not sure. I think it's what happens when it rains and they have the top down."

✶ ✶ ✶

What happens to car mufflers when they grow old?

  They constantly feel exhausted.

✶ ✶ ✶

TONGUE TWISTER

Moses supposes his toeses are roses,
But Moses supposes erroneously.
For nobody's toeses are poses of roses.
As Moses supposes his toeses to be.

BEARS

What's large, white, fierce, eats salmon, and lives in the Sahara Desert?
The polar bear that got lost.

✳ ✳ ✳

Where do bears like to stay when they go on vacation?
At cave-inns.

✳ ✳ ✳

"My feet are sore," one bear said to another. "I'm going to the mall to buy tennis shoes."

"What for?" asked his friend. "You're still going to have bear feet."

Brad: "Why do bears paint their faces yellow?"

Lad: "Don't know."

Brad: "So they can hide in banana trees."

Lad: "Impossible. I've never seen a bear in a banana tree."

Brad: "That's because they've painted their faces yellow."

✳ ✳ ✳

What's black and white, black and white, black and white?

A panda bear rolling down the mountain.

✳ ✳ ✳

Where do bears get their news?

From cub reporters.

✳ ✳ ✳

Why does a bear sleep three months out of the year?

No one is brave enough to wake it up.

"Someone's been eating my soup!" shouted Papa Bear.

"Someone's been eating my soup!" shouted Mama Bear.

"Hooray!" shouted Baby Bear. "Does that mean we can have ice cream for supper?"

✳ ✳ ✳

"Someone's been eating my soup!" yelled Papa Bear, finding his bowl empty at the supper table.

"And someone's been eating my soup!" yelled Baby Bear. His bowl was empty, too.

"Stop fussing," said Mama Bear. "I'm still cooking it."

✳ ✳ ✳

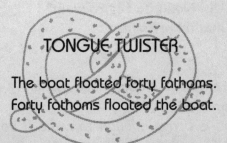

TONGUE TWISTER

The boat floated forty fathoms.
Forty fathoms floated the boat.

BIBLE JOKES

"Who was the fastest runner in history?" asked Shelley.

"Adam," said Mackie. "The Bible says he was first in the human race."

* * *

What did Noah do for a living?

He was an ark-itect.

* * *

Science Teacher: "Who discovered oxygen?"
Student: "Adam."

"Why does God create all humans as babies?" asked Bob. "Why doesn't He just go ahead and make us adults?"

"I suppose it's because babies take less material," suggested Toby.

* * *

"Do you think the worms on Noah's Ark were allowed to live inside apples?" asked Gigi.

"Oh, no," said Honi. "They had to be in pairs, remember?"

* * *

"Does God hear everything in the world?" asked a Sunday school student.

"Yes," the teacher said, "every sound."

"All at one time?"

"Yes."

"Wow. His ears must be hurting from all that noise on the radio."

When do we first read of baseball in the Bible?

Genesis 1:1. It starts, "In the Big Inning. . . ."

✳ ✳ ✳

"Mom and Dad say we can't go to the zoo today," sighed Barbie.

"I have an idea," suggested Joan. "We can go over their heads. Let's pray!"

✳ ✳ ✳

Sunday School Teacher: "Who was Noah's wife?"

Student: "Er . . . Joan of Ark?"

✳ ✳ ✳

Who was the most popular Old Testament actor?

Samson, who brought down the house.

BIRDS

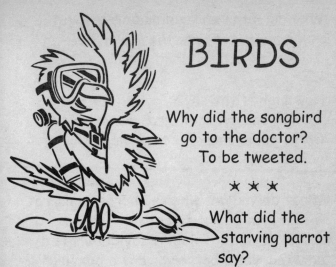

Why did the songbird
go to the doctor?
To be tweeted.

* * *

What did the
starving parrot
say?
Polly wanna *CHEESEBURGER!*

* * *

Amanda went to the pet store and told the
clerk, "I want a BIG bag of bird seed."

"You must be planning to feed a lot of
sparrows," said the clerk.

"No, actually, I'm planning to dye the seed
blue and plant a BIG crop of bluebirds."

Why does the egret stand on one leg?
Because if it lifts the leg, it falls.

✷ ✷ ✷

How high is the sky?
High enough that birds don't have to worry about bumping their heads.

✷ ✷ ✷

What do you get when you cross a parrot with a man-eating tiger?
Not sure. But when it says it wants a cracker, you'd better give it a boxful!

✷ ✷ ✷

"That's the biggest bird I've ever seen!"
"It's only a swallow."
"Swallow? That's more like a gulp!"

✷ ✷ ✷

What is a bird's favorite food?
Chocolate chirp cookies.

Teacher: "What kinds of birds are commonly found in jungles?"
Student: "Hot, sweaty birds."

✶ ✶ ✶

"My parakeet has proposed marriage," said Roger.

"Who does it want to marry?" asked Drew.

"Its childhood tweetheart."

✶ ✶ ✶

"What kinds of birds are the best protectors?" asked the teacher.

"The knightingale and the knight owl," answered the student.

✶ ✶ ✶

Why were the birds punished?

For using fowl language.

BROTHERS & SISTERS

"We're playing school,"
said sis. "Wanna join us?"
"Sure," said brother.
"I'm out sick today."

* * *

"Who is your brother?"
asked the new minister.

"No, Who is not my brother," corrected
Misty. "My brother's name is Patrick."

* * *

"Why is little sister crying?" Mom called
down the hallway.

"She tried to go downstairs without walking," big sister answered.

Dad: "Where are your ice skates?"

Laurence: "I let sister use them."

Dad: "That was very nice of you. Where is she now?"

Laurence: "She's out on the lake, checking to see if the ice is thick enough."

✳ ✳ ✳

"Dad, I'm tired of sleepwalking," said Caleb. "What can I do?"

"Well, let's put your tricycle in your bedroom."

✳ ✳ ✳

"I couldn't sleep last night," said brother.

"Why not?" asked sister.

"I had this dream that the sun had disappeared and wasn't coming back."

"That's ridiculous. You lay awake all night worrying about that?"

"Yeah. Then finally, just a little while ago, it dawned on me. . . ."

"My parents just got a new computer for my teen-age sister," said Jon.

"I wish my parents could make that kind of trade for my big sister," said Ron.

✶ ✶ ✶

"Mom, I want a pet skunk," said Tricia.

"And where, exactly, do you propose to keep it?"

"In brother's room."

"What would he do about the terrible odor?"

"I'm sure the skunk's used to it."

✶ ✶ ✶

"I really am brilliant," boasted Wylie.

"Prove it," said his brother Bing.

"See that picture puzzle on the table? I finished it all by myself in just three weeks."

"What's so great about that?"

"The box says five to seven years."

Kristin: "Why can't your sister Linda come out and play with us?"

Andie: "She has phonesia."

Kristin: "What in the world is phonesia?"

Andie: "She's being punished for tying up the phone all night long."

✳ ✳ ✳

"Mom, we think you're fantastic," said Jan. "You're so understanding, and loving, and caring, and organized, and well-dressed— and the greatest cook in America."

"Yeah," agreed Kathy. "We're planning to build you a mom-ument!"

✳ ✳ ✳

"You must share your cookies with your little brother," mother scolded Suella. "Why, even chickens and sparrows know the importance of sharing food."

"If we were talking about worms," Suella said, "there would be *no problem*!"

"What's this?" asked brother.

"It's dessert. I made it," said sister.

"What do you call it?"

"That's pound cake, silly!"

"Oh. I can see why."

"What do you mean?"

"I'll need a hammer to pound out the lumps."

✳ ✳ ✳

"My sister always tiptoes past the medicine cabinet."

"Why so quiet?"

"She doesn't wanna wake up the sleeping pills."

✳ ✳ ✳

"*Oooo!* This wind is terrible," said sis. "It's made a total mess of my hair."

"Yeah," agreed brother. "You look like you've been through a hairicane."

Dee: I've made the tuna casserole
Dum: Good. I thought it was for us.

★ ★ ★

Dee: This ointment makes my leg smart.
Dum: Well, why not rub some on your head?

★ ★ ★

Dee: Who gave you that black eye?
Dum: Nobody. I had to fight for it!

★ ★ ★

TONGUE TWISTER

Sue sued Sukie for Sukie's new blue shoes.
Sukie sued Sue for Sue's gooey blue glue.
If Sue sued Sukie and Sukie sued Sue,
Who has the new gooey glued blue shoes?

CATS

"Dad's mad at the cat," said Kristin. "What did the cat do now?" asked John. "Dad discovered she's been driving the car at night."

* * *

Why couldn't the cat slip through the eye of a needle?

Someone tied a knot in its tail.

* * *

"What is your cat's favorite food?" asked David.

"Mice cream," said Micah.

34

What do you call the grandfather of a kitten?

A grandpaw.

✶ ✶ ✶

How did the kitten get to the top of the tree?

It stood on an acorn and waited for it to grow.

✶ ✶ ✶

What kind of cars do kittens drive?

Catillacs.

✶ ✶ ✶

"Jack, put out the cat," Mother instructed as the family got ready for bed.

"I can't, Mom."

"Why not?"

"Because it hasn't come in all day."

CHICKENS, TURKEYS, ETC.

How do young chicks escape from their eggs?
Through the eggs-its.

* * *

If chickens never really fly, why do they have wings?
So we can distinguish them from horses.

* * *

What do chickens have to be thankful for on Thanksgiving Day?
The fact that they're not turkeys.

What disease do chickens dread the worst?
  Peoplepox.

* * *

Why did the turkey cross the road?
  It saw the Pilgrims sailing in.

* * *

Why did the Easter bunny cross the road?
  To escape the angry children who couldn't find all the hidden eggs.

* * *

What do chickens do at Kentucky Fried Chicken?
  They kick the bucket.

* * *

Why did the kangaroo decide not to cross the road?
  It didn't want to be called a chicken.

Why did the chicken cross the playground?
To get to the other slide.

* * *

TONGUE TWISTER

If rustlers wrestle wrestlers
While rustlers rustle rustles,
Could rustlers rustle wrestlers
While wrestlers wrestle rustlers?

COMPUTERS

How did the computer criminal get out of jail?
Pressed the <Escape> key.

* * *

What is the favorite snack of computer programmers?
Chips.

* * *

"Did you hear about the spider that enrolled in computer courses?"
"Yeah. It wanted to learn to design Web pages."

What does the baby computer call its daddy?

Da-ta.

* * *

What's an astronaut's favorite part of a computer?

The spacebar.

* * *

Why did the computer get up and leave the office?

To go have a byte of lunch.

* * *

Teacher: "Who was the first American president to use a computer?"

Student: "Warren G. Hard Drive."

* * *

Why did the computer die?

It had a terminal illness.

"Did you hear about the computer that went to the doctor complaining of a chronic cough?"
"No. What was the diagnosis?"
"It had come down with a virus."

✳ ✳ ✳

How do you catch computer hackers?
With mousetraps.

✳ ✳ ✳

What kind of computers wear shades?
The ones that have Windows.

✳ ✳ ✳

What devices do White House officials use to navigate with computers?
White mice.

✳ ✳ ✳

How are computers like soldiers?
They all have to boot up.

How do computer spiders catch computer bugs?

They trap them on the World Wide Web.

* * *

Where do the really cool mice hang out?

In mousepads.

* * *

What do you call two Internet users who get married?

Newlywebs.

* * *

What did the computer programmers have for a little snack?

Microchips.

COPS & ROBBERS

What do you call a police detective who solves computer crimes?

A hacker tracker.

* * *

"I think we should rob the Blackstones' house tomorrow night while they're out of town," one burglar said to his partner.

"You're crazy," said the partner. "They must have half a dozen dogs. The barking will wake up the whole neighborhood."

"Nah, I have it figured differently. The dogs will be barking so loudly, nobody will hear us break the window."

"What are you in for?" one prison inmate asked another.

"Robbed a grocery store."

"How much did you get?"

"About $1,500."

"How'd you get caught?"

"Couldn't get away fast enough."

"Why not?"

"The money bags were too heavy. It was all in nickels and pennies."

* * *

Why was the butcher arrested?

The police caught him chop-lifting.

* * *

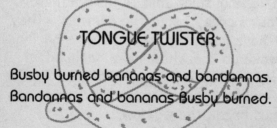

TONGUE TWISTER

Busby burned bananas and bandannas.
Bandannas and bananas Busby burned.

COWS

How can you guarantee milk won't go sour?
Don't milk the cow.

✳ ✳ ✳

Why did the cow cross the road?
To see what was on the udder side.

✳ ✳ ✳

What animal says "oom"?
A backward cow.

✳ ✳ ✳

What do you call a cow eating grass in your yard?
A lawn moo-er.

"If a cow's head is pointed west, in which direction is its tail pointed?" Wade asked.

"East," said Wyatt.

"No," said Wade. "It's pointed down."

✷ ✷ ✷

"I understand your bull wins first prize at the state fair each year," a stranger said to farmer Jackson.

"That's right," said the farmer.

"What do you figure that bull's worth?" asked the stranger.

"Depends."

"What do you mean?"

"Depends on whether you wanna buy him or tax me for him."

✷ ✷ ✷

What do you hear when cows start singing?

Moo-sic.

DEFINITIONS

ant: *an industrious insect that works hardest when it's at a picnic.*

✱ ✱ ✱

arcade: *what everyone on Noah's ark drank.*

✱ ✱ ✱

bagel: *a gull that prefers the bay to the sea.*

✱ ✱ ✱

blooming idiots: *flowers that are stupid in springtime.*

✱ ✱ ✱

bookworm: *a highly educated worm.*

board of education: *the school principal's paddle.*

* * *

brainstorm: *Albert Einstein being struck on the head by lightning.*

* * *

budget: *something that's impossible for an 8-year-old to do with a thousand-pound rock.*

* * *

butter: *an aggressive billy goat.*

* * *

candlemaker: *someone who works wick ends.*

* * *

canteen: *a thirst-aid container.*

* * *

cobwebs: *what you find if you don't use the World Wide Web for a few days.*

coronet: *the coroner's daughter.*

★ ★ ★

cross-examination: *a pop quiz given by a mean teacher.*

★ ★ ★

debate: *what you stick on a hook to attract de fish.*

★ ★ ★

decayed: *a period of 10 years.*

★ ★ ★

deer antler: *opposite of deer uncler.*

★ ★ ★

dynamite: *a cross between a dinosaur and a termite.*

★ ★ ★

echo: *something grown-ups can't punish for talking back.*

electric bill: *what a duck gets when it runs into a wall socket.*

✶ ✶ ✶

electrician: *someone who's always wiring for more money.*

✶ ✶ ✶

enchilada: *an inch-long lada.*

✶ ✶ ✶

evergreen: *opposite of nevergreen.*

✶ ✶ ✶

farm: *a place where you work from day-break 'til backbreak.*

✶ ✶ ✶

fjord: *a kind of automobile in Norway.*

✶ ✶ ✶

flashlight: *a plastic or metal container for dead batteries.*

flower: *something that achieves great success by staying in beds.*

★ ★ ★

flyswatter: *a device that grows at the end of cows.*

★ ★ ★

friend: *someone who knows everything about you but likes you anyway.*

★ ★ ★

goose: *a fowl that has to grow up in order to grow down.*

★ ★ ★

grandfather clock: *an old timer.*

★ ★ ★

Greece: *a substance used for frying food.*

ground beef: *cattle that graze on grass—as opposed to water beef.*

* * *

hardships: *the way the Pilgrims came to America.*

* * *

headlines: *marks left by corduroy pillows.*

* * *

historian: *someone who just can't let the past lie.*

* * *

holiday: *when a famous person has a birthday and they close the schools!*

* * *

horse: *an oats-mobile.*

* * *

icycles: *the way snowmen travel.*

indigestion: *what happens when a square meal is too large to fit into an oval stomach.*

* * *

infinity: *the place where two parallel lines never meet.*

* * *

jail: *a key club.*

* * *

jet-setter: *a breed of dog that can fly 600 miles an hour at 30,000 feet.*

* * *

kneecap: *a hat for covering your knee.*

* * *

lap: *the part of you that never stands up.*

* * *

leopard: *the animal that's easiest to spot.*

light snack: *a candy-coated candle.*

★ ★ ★

lobster: *a tennis player who chops every shot.*

★ ★ ★

maneuver: *what farmers put on early crops to help them grow.*

★ ★ ★

medieval: *the period in history when everybody was half bad.*

★ ★ ★

misfortune: *daughter of Mr. and Mrs. Fortune.*

★ ★ ★

mixed emotions: *the kind of feeling you get when your mom comes to get you out of school early in order to take you to the dentist.*

moonlight: *nighttime sunlight.*

* * *

moth: *husband of a myth.*

* * *

mountain climber: *an athlete with the gift of grab.*

* * *

net income: *what a fisherman gets paid.*

* * *

nightmare: *a horse that prefers to roam at night.*

* * *

"Nutcracker Suite": *where The Chipmunks stay when they're on tour.*

* * *

pendulum: *the swingingest part of a clock.*

penguin: *the animal that always wears a tuxedo.*

* * *

petrified wood: *a frightened log.*

* * *

pharmacy: *where people learn how to pharm.*

* * *

pimple: *opposite of dimple.*

* * *

popcorn: *father of childcorn.*

* * *

prizefight: *a squabble over a Cracker Jacks box.*

* * *

professional golfer: *a person who earns a living by playing a round.*

56

revolving door: *where strangers often meet and go around together.*

* * *

riverbank: *where tadpoles save their money.*

* * *

rubber band: *musical bicycle tires.*

* * *

rustler: *a thief looking for beef.*

* * *

skeleton: *a body with the inside out and the outside missing.*

* * *

sleet: *precipitation that can't decide whether it wants to be rain or snow.*

* * *

smile: *a curve that can straighten out a lot of problems.*

snowball: *where snowmen and snowwomen dance.*

* * *

square: *a circle with corners.*

* * *

steel wool: *what sheep thieves do.*

* * *

stick: *a boomerang that won't return.*

* * *

stock exchange: *the place were cows are traded.*

* * *

stoplight: *opposite of golight.*

* * *

submarine: *a can of people.*

sunspots: *symptoms that the sun has chicken-pox.*

* * *

sweater: *something you have to put on when Mom gets cold.*

* * *

sycamore tree: *the sickest tree in the forest.*

* * *

thumbtacks: *a tax imposed on hitchhikers.*

* * *

transparent: *a train's father or mother.*

* * *

vacuum cleaner: *a broom with a stomach.*

* * *

vicious circle: *the meanest part of geometry class.*

59

violinist: *a musician who does nothing but fiddle around.*

✷ ✷ ✷

vitamin: *what you should do when your grandparents ring your doorbell.*

✷ ✷ ✷

volcano: *a mountain with burning indigestion.*

✷ ✷ ✷

waffle: *a pancake with treads.*

✷ ✷ ✷

watchdog: *a dog that can tell time.*

✷ ✷ ✷

webbing: *the happy occasion when spiders get married.*

✷ ✷ ✷

wig: *a convertible top.*

wombat: *what you use to strike at a wom-ball.*

✳ ✳ ✳

woodpecker: *the knockingbird.*

✳ ✳ ✳

yardstick: *something that has a third foot but still can't crawl, walk or run.*

✳ ✳ ✳

zoo: *a jail for animals.*

✳ ✳ ✳

TONGUE TWISTER

Sliver hither, Zither!

Sneaky thieves seized the skis.

THE DOCTOR

"My son says he feels like an apple," Mother told the doctor. "I don't understand what's wrong with him."

"Well, bring him on in for a check-up," said the doctor. "I won't bite him."

* * *

"Doc, I need a prescription."

"For yourself?"

"No, it's for my fireplace."

"Your fireplace? What seems to be the trouble?"

"I think it has the flue."

What did the elevator say to the doctor?
  "I'm coming down with something."

* * *

Dental Patient: "How much would you charge to pull that bad tooth of mine?"
Dentist: "Our regular rate for pulling teeth: $75."
Patient: "Well, how much would you charge to loosen it for me?"

* * *

"Doctor, I think I'm sick," said the alligator.
  "That makes you an illigator," said the doctor.

* * *

"Doctor," screamed a caller on the phone, "I've just swallowed a camera with a roll of film in it."
  "Well, just sit tight," the doctor said. "Let's wait and see what develops."

Patient: "What do you want?"

Nurse: "I came to take your blood pressure."

Patient: "I need it. Use your own blood pressure."

✳ ✳ ✳

Why did the window have to be taken to the doctor's office?

It was suffering from windowpanes.

✳ ✳ ✳

Why did the stand-up comic go see the doctor?

She had tired feet.

✳ ✳ ✳

How can a surgeon tell whether a patient is a librarian or an electrician?

The heart, lungs, liver, kidneys and stomach of a librarian are all numbered. The insides of an electrician are color-coded.

"Doctor, my tooth is loose."

   "Try gluing it with toothpaste."

∗ ∗ ∗

"How can I stop this nosebleed?" a patient asked.

   "Hold your breath until your heart stops beating," said the doctor.

∗ ∗ ∗

"Well, I believe we've solved your little hearing problem with these hearing aids," the doctor said. "That will be $900."

   The patient pretended not to hear, and walked out the door.

∗ ∗ ∗

"My neck hurts every time I turn my head," complained the patient. "What should I do?"

   "Don't turn your head," recommended the doctor.

The doctor was trying to cheer Artie, who'd sprained his wrist. "When you get out of this sling," the doctor told him, "you'll feel better than ever. You'll be able to write, catch Frisbees, and bounce basketballs with the best of them."

Artie stopped crying and brightened up. "Wow!" he said. "I've never been able to bounce a basketball before!"

✳ ✳ ✳

"How do you feel?" asked the doctor.

"Like a dog," moaned Katie.

"Well, sit," the doctor said. "Stay."

✳ ✳ ✳

"Doc, there's something wrong with my soda crackers."

"What are the symptoms?"

"They feel crumby."

"Doctor, my ear won't stop ringing."
　"Then answer it."

★ ★ ★

TONGUE TWISTER

Chip chopped chuck
　for chipped chuck soup
Chipped chuck soup was
　chopped by Chip.

DOGS

"Mom, the dog bit sister's hand again!"

"Uh-oh. We'd better take a look. We may need to put something on it."

"Nah, I think the dog prefers her hand plain."

* * *

Why did the dog refuse to wear its wrist-watch?

Because the watch had ticks.

* * *

Why do firemen have dogs for mascots?

To help them locate the fire hydrants.

Myra: "Our dog must be older than we thought."

Luke: "What makes you think so?"

Myra: "She's started bringing in yesterday's newspaper."

＊ ＊ ＊

"We had to buy our dog a longer leash," Zan said.

"Why?" asked Van.

"Dad kept stepping on its tail."

＊ ＊ ＊

"What do you think of my police dog?"

"Dog? That animal says 'meoww'!"

"Yes. It's working undercover at the moment."

＊ ＊ ＊

What sign did the bulldog put in front of its doghouse?

BEWARE OF RESIDENT.

"What's your dog's name?"

"Ginger, when she's not biting people."

"What's her name when she *is* biting people?"

"Ginger Snaps."

✳ ✳ ✳

"Do you think Dottie's clean?" asked Myra, bringing her Dalmatian to show Mom after bathing the dog.

"Yes," Mom said, inspecting the ears and paws. "She's pretty clean."

"Actually," said Myra, "I think she's pretty even when she's dirty."

✳ ✳ ✳

What do you call a nature film about dogs?

Dog-umentaries.

✳ ✳ ✳

At what point in history were dogs happiest?

During the Bone Age.

Who do dogs mail their Christmas wish lists to?

   Santa Paws.

★ ★ ★

A movie screenwriter waited eagerly for word on whether her latest work had been accepted by any of the film companies. She hounded her agent every day. Finally, the agent phoned her to report.

   "Good news," the agent said. "Warner Brothers loved your script and literally ate it up."

   "That's wonderful!" beamed the screenwriter. "So when will they be making the movie?"

   "Well, there's one small problem. Warner Brothers is my dog. . . ."

★ ★ ★

What do you call it when two dogs negotiate?

   Flea bargaining.

"My dog knows how to wash my clothes for me," said Chip.

"Is that what you call a 'laundromutt'?" asked Trip.

✳ ✳ ✳

The Johnstons invited their new neighbors the Andersons for dinner. Everyone was having a great time, enjoying the food and conversation. Mr. Anderson was curious, though, to observe that the Johnstons' dog sat right beside him on the floor and stared at him the whole evening.

"This is a very nice dog you have," Mr. Anderson said. "But I wonder why he keeps looking at me like that."

"Probably," the Johnstons' little boy suggested, "it's because you're eating off of his plate."

"If you were being chased by two German shepherds," posed Erin, "what steps would you take?"

"Long ones," said Bart.

★ ★ ★

"Does your dog Dolly have fleas?" asked Brianne.

"No—but she just had puppies!" said Erica.

★ ★ ★

TONGUE TWISTER

Eight bright lights.
Great bright nights.

ELEPHANTS

How do you stop an elephant from chasing you? *With elephant repellent.*

* * *

Two children were at the zoo.
"Elephants sure are fat animals," commented one.

"Yeah. I guess my mom was right when she said peanuts are fattening."

* * *

William: "I can stop a charging elephant with one hand."
Pete: "I don't believe an elephant with one hand would be charging."

How does an elephant get down a chimney?
    It volunteers as one of Santa's helpers and hides in the toy sack.

✳ ✳ ✳

Why do most elephants look fat?
    They go to inexperienced tailors.

✳ ✳ ✳

How do you trap an elephant?
    Take a big net, hide in the jungle and sound like a peanut.

✳ ✳ ✳

What's huge, gray, has a trunk and goes up and down?
    An elephant on an elevator.

✳ ✳ ✳

What wears beautiful slippers and weighs several tons?
    Cinderelephant.

What do you get when you cross an elephant with an overloaded computer?

A crash through the jungle.

★ ★ ★

If an elephant falls into a cup of coffee, what's the result?

Death by drowning. Elephants don't swim well in coffee.

★ ★ ★

What's gray and red, weighs 4,000 pounds, and has two trunks and eight legs?

Two elephants wearing red bikinis.

★ ★ ★

What do you get when you cross an elephant with peanut butter?

An elephant that sticks to the roof of your mouth.

What kind of vegetable do you find under elephants' feet?

Squash.

✶ ✶ ✶

What did the elephants wear at the swimming pool?

Trunks.

✶ ✶ ✶

Teacher: "Which is taller—an elephant or a giraffe?"

Student: "They're both the same height."

Teacher: "You're forgetting that the giraffe has that very long neck. That means when it raises its head, it has greater height."

Student: "Yes, but their feet all go to the exact same depth."

FAMOUS CHARACTERS

Who loves to solve mysteries and soak in bubble baths?
Sherlock Foams.

★ ★ ★

Mike: "What do you do for a living?"
Harve: "I get fired every day."
Mike: "How can you earn a living by getting
fired every day?"
Harve: "I'm the star of the circus. I'm the
guy they call the Human Cannonball."

Humpty Dumpty sat on a wall.
　　Humpty Dumpty had a great fall. . .
　　but winter wasn't much to speak of.

✱ ✱ ✱

Teacher: "What is Abraham Lincoln most
　　famous for?"
Student: "The $5 bill."

✱ ✱ ✱

Brit and his family were about to take off
on an airplane.
　　"You need to buckle your seatbelt now,"
his dad said.
　　"But I'm Superman," Brit complained. "I
don't need to wear a seatbelt."
　　"If you were Superman, you wouldn't need
an airplane, either."

✱ ✱ ✱

What do you call Batman after he's been
flattened by a steamroller?
　　Flatman.

Who makes a sound like "ninety-nine-THUMP, ninety-nine-THUMP" when he walks?

   Long John Centipede.

★ ★ ★

"Did you hear about Vincent Van Gogh's cousin who started the stagecoach line?"
   "No. What was his name?"
   "Wells Far Gogh."

★ ★ ★

"Did you hear about Van Gogh's other cousin who was a famous lady magician?"
   "No. What was her name?"
   "Where Didshe Gogh."

FARM LIFE

Alvin: "Wow, that scarecrow sure is scary!"
Marvin: "Yeah, I bet the birds are so scared they bring back the food they took last year."

* * *

What's a lamb's favorite meat sauce?
Baa-baa-que sauce.

* * *

Where do gardeners mail their letters?
At the nearest U.S. Compost Office.

"Do you think we should buy a horse or a cow with our harvest money this autumn?" a farmer asked his wife.

"Well, the neighbors sure would laugh at you if they saw you trying to milk a horse."

"That's true. Of course, they'd laugh at me if they saw me trying to ride a cow, too."

✱ ✱ ✱

Why should you never tell a secret in a cornfield?

Because the stalks have ears.

✱ ✱ ✱

What did the farmer do when he finally caught the stray pig?

Put it in hamcuffs.

✱ ✱ ✱

Why was the farmer so stressed out?

He was studying for the soil test.

"Daddy, what will we do with the hog after we butcher it?" asked the farm lad.

"Then we cure the meat."

The boy scratched his head. "Don't we have things backward, daddy?"

"What do you mean, son?"

"Well, it seems to me that if we're gonna try to cure it, we should do that while the hog's still alive."

★ ★ ★

"What's the name of your hog?"

"Ballpoint."

"Why do you call it Ballpoint?"

"Actually, that's just its pen name."

★ ★ ★

"My dad grows corn so big he gets three dollars an ear at market," said one farm lad.

"That's nothing," said his friend. "My dad grows cantaloupe so big it takes only three to make a dozen."

"How have you been doing?" asked Farmer Smith.

"Not too well," said Farmer Brown. "I just got out of the hospital."

"Land sakes! What was wrong?"

"I was kicked in the head by my old mule."

"What a terrible accident!"

"Wasn't an accident. I reckon the mule did it on purpose."

* * *

"My farmer cousin just got back from vacation. It was the first time he'd taken a break from farming in more than ten years."

"Where did he go?"

"To the beach."

"Oh, he must have enjoyed that!"

"He sure did. He was a little disappointed with surfing, though. The tractor engine kept choking down in the surf."

What happened when the pig pen broke?
The pig had to start using a pencil.

* * *

What did the farmer say when he found a hole in one of his pumpkins?
"I think I need a pumpkin patch."

* * *

What's the difference between a granary and a grandpa?
One's a corn bin. The other's your born kin.

* * *

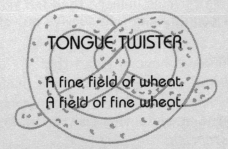

TONGUE TWISTER

A fine field of wheat.
A field of fine wheat.

FISH

Kippie: "I caught a
fish yesterday
that weighed ten
pounds!"
Mickie: "I don't
believe it."
Kippie: "It's true.
The picture alone weighed almost a pound."

* * *

In what country can fish survive out of
water?
Finland.

* * *

What's the most famous fish in the world?
The starfish.

"Jerry, I insist that you take your little brother fishing with you," Dad said sternly.

"But dad, he—"

"No buts. He needs to learn how to fish, and you can teach him while I'm busy here in the shop."

"But dad, he—"

"I told you, no buts. Now go."

"But there's no bait."

"What do you mean? I just bought you a box of crickets."

"Little brother has already eaten 'em all."

✳ ✳ ✳

What did the fish boat captain say to the card magician?

Pick a cod, any cod.

✳ ✳ ✳

What are the first things fish learn in school?

Their A-B-Seas.

Who are hammerhead sharks' best friends?
  Nailhead sharks.

✱ ✱ ✱

"I keep my goldfish in a huge tank," said Mark.
  "I keep mine in the bathtub," said Mitch.
  "In the bathtub? What do you do with them when you need to take a bath?"
  "I make them cover their eyes."

✱ ✱ ✱

"You can't catch fish here," the game warden told Timmy. "You don't have a license."
  "Well, I haven't had a bite all day," Timmy said. "I doubt I could catch fish here even if I did have a license."

✱ ✱ ✱

Why do goldfish have to be kept inside?
  Because they'll slip through the leash if you try to take them out for a walk.

What are tropical fishes' favorite foods?
  Reef-fried beans.

✳ ✳ ✳

Two boys were walking home from the creek with a nice string of fish. They'd had a great day fishing, but their prizes were starting to emit a strong, unpleasant odor.

"I sure wish there was some way we could keep 'em from smelling," said one boy.

"Well," said the other, "I reckon we could clamp their noses."

✳ ✳ ✳

How do you catch a school of fish?
  With a bookworm.

✳ ✳ ✳

Blake: "We're not catching any fish. Why don't you tell them to start biting?"
Jake: "How can I communicate with a fish?"
Blake: "Drop them another line."

FOOD

What did one blueberry say to the other?
  "You sure got us into a jam this time."

* * *

What's the favorite food of astronauts?
  Launch meat.

* * *

What do you call a lazy butcher?
  A meatloafer.

What did the strawberry do when it couldn't get a date for the breakfast dance?

It invited a raisin.

* * *

"Mother, that's your third helping of eggs!"

"I love eggs, dear. They're good for you."

"But I'm afraid you're going to turn into a momelette!"

* * *

What becomes of cabbage and carrots if you accidentally store them in the freezer instead of the refrigerator?

They turn into cold slaw.

* * *

"Oooo!" shrieked Clark. "This cheese is dreadful! It has holes in it!"

"Never mind that," his mother said. "Just eat the cheese. You don't have to eat the holes today."

"Breakfast this morning was out of this world," said Mollie.

"What did you have?" teased Dollie. "Flying sausages?"

* * *

Mother: "Valerie, why are you staring at the frozen grapefruit container?"
Valerie: "Because it says CONCENTRATE."

* * *

What did the cake batter say to the spatula?
"*Stop stirring at me!*"

* * *

"How much do you like spinach?"
"Actually, I like nothing better."

* * *

What food do you find on the honor roll?
Brilliant butter.

"Oh, no, not fried chicken," moaned little Cindy, coming into the kitchen for dinner. "I don't think I can *stand* to eat fried chicken this evening!"

"Why not?" asked her mother. "You liked it last night and the night before that, and the night before that. . . ."

* * *

What's a miner's favorite food?
Coal slaw.

* * *

"My Mom sure gets mean when she's in the kitchen," Scot said.

"What does she do?" asked Branden.

"She does things like beat the cake mix, mash the potatoes, whip the cream. . . ."

* * *

What's a puppy's favorite pizza topping?
Pupperoni.

What kind of cheese makes the best building material?

Cottage cheese.

✳ ✳ ✳

What can you always find to eat if you're shipwrecked on a deserted island?

Lots of SAND-wiches.

✳ ✳ ✳

What kind of food comes in a can and doesn't make a sound?

Corned-beef hush.

✳ ✳ ✳

What national park is famous for its desserts?

Jellystone.

✳ ✳ ✳

How do you repair a strawberry?

With a strawberry patch.

What made the pickle so sour?
  It had a jarring ordeal.

* * *

What flying machine is good to eat?
  The jellycopter.

* * *

"Where can I get a chicken dinner cheap?"
  "Try the feed store."

* * *

"Where are you going?" one slice of bread asked another.
  "I'm going to mail this postcard."
  "But bread slices can't mail postcards."
  "Sure we can. That's what the toast office is there for."

* * *

A woman returned to the supermarket with her nine bags of groceries and a long receipt. She demanded to see the store manager.

"What's the problem?" the manager asked.

"You can see right here on the receipt that I paid for two TV dinners," the woman fumed. "So where's the TV?"

✳ ✳ ✳

What's the difference between a moldy vegetable and a depressing song?

One is a bad salad, and the other is a sad ballad.

✳ ✳ ✳

TONGUE TWISTER

Does Steve still strew straw
in the still straw stall?

FROGS

How do frogs handle stress?

When something bugs them, they simply eat it.

* * *

"My pet frog can work math problems," bragged Buster.

"No way," said Bryce. "Show me."

Buster held his frog in his palm and asked it, "What's ten minus ten?"

And the frog said nothing.

The question on the biology test asked:
"Name three kinds of frogs."

The student wrote: "daddy frog, mama frog, baby frog."

✲ ✲ ✲

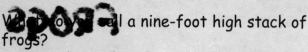l a nine-foot high stack of frogs?

A toadem pole.

✲ ✲ ✲

What kind of shoes do frogs wear?

Open-toad slippers.

✲ ✲ ✲

What's the best way to clear frogs off your car windows?

With the defrogger.

✲ ✲ ✲

"Let's go see a movie," suggested one frog to another.

"Okay. I hope it has a hoppy ending."

What do you get when you cross a frog and a chair?
   A toadstool.

★ ★ ★

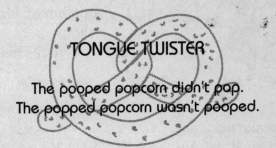

TONGUE TWISTER

The pooped popcorn didn't pop.
The popped popcorn wasn't pooped.

GROWN-UPS

What did Dad
write on the
bottom of his
shoe?

A footnote.

✳ ✳ ✳

"Did you take a shower
this morning, son?"

"No, Mom. Are we missing one?"

✳ ✳ ✳

"Mom, I have a stomachache."

"I don't doubt it. You hardly touched your
lunch, and you only picked at your dinner.
When your stomach is empty, it lets you
know by aching."

"So when you complain of a headache,
does that mean your head's empty?"

A woman hurried inside a beauty shop mopping her face with a handkerchief. "It must be ninety degrees outside," she told the cosmetologist. "Can you give me some hair-conditioning?"

*** *** ***

"You look so cute when you're asleep," mother said, tucking Cassie into bed.

"Thanks, Mom, but I wouldn't know," said Cassie.

*** *** ***

Two fathers were discussing their children, who were in college.

"My daughter will graduate next May," said one proudly. "Then she plans to start work as an engineer."

"I'm not sure when my son will graduate," said the other father dejectedly.

"Well, what do expect he'll be when he does graduate?"

"I expect he'll be a senior citizen."

"I'm never going to get married," Belinda announced.

"Why not?" asked her friend.

"I just don't need a husband. I already have a father who snores, a mother who takes out the garbage and a brother with stinky feet."

* * *

Mack: "Man, I really was in hot water last night after coming home all muddy from the river."

Zack: "Me, too. My mom made me take a bath."

* * *

"Mom, may I have a snare drum?"

"Definitely not. Those things are far too loud for the peace and quiet of the neighborhood."

"But mom, I promise I'll only play it while everyone's asleep."

Dad opened the monthly electric bill and almost fainted when he saw the amount. "This," he groaned, "is what I call a shock!"

* * *

Josh: "My dad manages a whole chain of convenience stores."

Mia: "What does a manager do?"

Josh: "Goes around and trains the staff, counts the money, checks the locks to see that everything is secure. Since they're all open twenty-four hours a day, every day of the year, that's a big responsibility."

Mia: "If they're open round the clock. . . why do they have locks?"

* * *

"I'm too tired to go to bed, even," Crystal said wearily to her dad.

"Well you'd better find some energy somewhere," her dad replied. "You're bed's not going to come to you."

"Grandma, how long have you been sewing?"

"Since I was about four years old."

"Wow! If I were you, I'd be bored by now!"

✳ ✳ ✳

"Oh, dear," grandmother said as she drove her grandchildren to school. "I just realized I've been speeding for the last several miles."

"Don't worry," piped up Al in the back seat. "The patrol car with the flashing lights behind you is doing the same speed, so it must be all right."

✳ ✳ ✳

A small child woke up his parents by hollering in the middle of the night.

"What is it?" his asked.

"There's a monster under my bed!"

Dad made his way to the closet in the dark. He opened and then slammed the closet door. "There," he said. "I've locked up the monster. Go back to sleep."

"Mom, what month of the year were you married in?"

"June."

"Dad, what month of the year were you married in?"

"June."

"Mom, what day of the week were you married on?"

"It was a Friday evening at 7 o'clock."

"Dad, what day of the week were you married on?"

"Friday at 7 p.m., same as your mother."

"Wow! Now *that's* what I call a coincidence!"

✳ ✳ ✳

"I reckon I know why parents and grandparents are called 'grown-ups'," said Travis.

"Why is that?" asked Mavis.

"Because they're always groaning."

"Mom, Barry just swallowed the remote control to the television set!"

"Well, then, go outside and ride your bikes for a while."

* * *

TONGUE TWISTER

The best breath test tests breath better.

Kick six sticks quick.

HISTORY

"Who became famous for inventing the cotton gin?" the teacher asked.

"A guy named Cotton," said the student.

* * *

"What can you tell us about the Iron Age?" asked the teacher.

The student thought a moment. "Well, I imagine things got pretty rusty after heavy rains."

* * *

How did medieval soldiers learn to fight?

They enrolled in knight classes.

Teacher: "What was the cause of the American Revolution?"

Student: "The traffic problem."

Teacher: "Traffic problem? There were no cars, trucks, or buses in those days. There were only horses and wagons."

Student: "But you said a few weeks ago that the colonists started the Revolution because they didn't like the king's taxis."

★ ★ ★

"What is believed to have happened to the people of the Stone Age?" asked the teacher.

"They were all petrified," said the student.

★ ★ ★

"Why did the early settlers wear three-cornered hats?" asked the history teacher.

"Because they had three-cornered heads?" Alison suggested.

108

Teacher: "What year was the Magna Carta signed?"

Student: "I don't know. That was long before I was born."

✳ ✳ ✳

Where have English kings and queens always been crowned?

On the head.

✳ ✳ ✳

History Teacher: "Why were the Middle Ages called the 'Dark Ages'?"

Student: "Because of all the knights."

✳ ✳ ✳

"Who were you named after?"

"George Washington."

"But your name is Bert."

"So what? I was named more than 200 years after they named George Washington."

Student: "Is it true that President Lincoln wrote the Gettysburg Address while riding from Washington to the battleground on the back of an envelope?"

Teacher: "Yes, that's what the history books tell us."

Student: "How many legs did the envelope have?"

✳ ✳ ✳

Teacher: "Who was John Paul Jones?"

Student: "He was a great American nasal hero."

✳ ✳ ✳

What did King Henry the Eighth and Popeye the Sailorman have in common?

Same middle name.

✳ ✳ ✳

"Who's your favorite leader of the Middle Ages?" the teacher asked.

"My Daddy!" said little Myra.

HORSES

Which side of a horse usually has the most hair?
The outside.

✶ ✶ ✶

Why do horses make such awkward dancers?
They have two left feet.

✶ ✶ ✶

"How's your sick horse?" one rancher asked another.
"She's in stable condition."

✶ ✶ ✶

Why did the rancher take the horse to the vet?
The horse had hay fever.

"Grandpa, why is it that horses can stand up and walk so much sooner after they're born than humans can?" Neil asked.

"Well, it's partly because they have twice as many legs as humans do, I suppose."

* * *

What kind of horse sees just as well with its tail as with its head?
A horse that's asleep.

* * *

What did one horse say to the other when they ran out of hay?
"Now that's the last straw!"

* * *

Alicia: "Do you know what it means when you find a horseshoe?"
Pat: "Yes. It means some poor horse probably has a sore foot by now."

INSECTS

"What's in style this season?" an insect asked a tailor.

"Yellow jackets."

* * *

Maria: "My school class has adopted a talking bird!"

Patsy: "That's nothing. My class has a spelling bee."

* * *

How do spiders prefer their corn?
   On the cobweb.

What kind of surgery is done in grasshopper hospitals?

Hoperations.

✱ ✱ ✱

What highways do dogs and cats hate most?

Fleaways.

✱ ✱ ✱

"It's New Year's Day," said one beetle to another. "Have you made any resolutions?"

"Yeah," said the other. "I'm gonna turn over a new leaf."

✱ ✱ ✱

Marie: "I think the ant is just the coolest animal! It works all day, effortlessly—and do you know how much it can get accomplished?"

Matt: "Yeah, a lot—until somebody steps on it."

"We have a real problem with biting insects around our yard," a customer told a pharmacist. "What can we do about it?"

"Stop biting them," suggested the pharmacist.

✱ ✱ ✱

What do bees like to chew?
Buzzlegum.

✱ ✱ ✱

When do ants travel fastest?
When they get on the anterstate highway.

✱ ✱ ✱

What are nature's busiest insects?
Fireflies. They're always on the glow.

✱ ✱ ✱

What kind of insects live on the moon?
Lunarticks.

Why do praying mantises have antennae?
   Cable service isn't available yet in their neighborhood.

★ ★ ★

How do snails get across oceans?
   In snailboats.

★ ★ ★

What kind of insect marries a ladybug?
   A gentlemanbug.

★ ★ ★

Stephanie: "Did you know I used to own a flea circus?"
Webster: "No. What happened to it?"
Stephanie: "A stray dog came along one day and stole the show."

★ ★ ★

What do you call an elderly ant?
   An ant-ique.

What's the difference between a bee and a fly?

You can't zip a bee.

* * *

Where do spiders turn when they need to know how to spell a word?

To Web-ster's Dictionary.

* * *

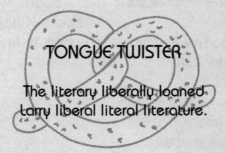

TONGUE TWISTER

The literary liberally loaned
Larry liberal literal literature.

KNOCK-KNOCK

Knock-knock.
Who's there?
Eddie.
Eddie Who?
Eddiebody who comes too close to me might catch my cold.

★ ★ ★

Knock-knock.
Who's there?
Maybe.
Maybe Who?
Maybe-bee gun is empty. Please sell may some more bee-bees.

118

Knock-knock.
Who's there?
Shorty.
Shorty Who?
Shorty Simmons, who can't reach the door-bell.

* * *

Knock-knock.
Who's there?
Pasture.
Pasture Who?
Pasture bedtime. Go to sleep.

* * *

Knock-knock.
Who's there?
Annie.
Annie Who?
Annie time you're ready come out and play, we're waiting on you.

Knock-knock.
  Who's there?
Europe.
  Europe Who?
Europe mighty early this morning.

★ ★ ★

Knock-knock.
  Who's there?
Atch.
  Atch who?
Sorry you have the cold.

★ ★ ★

Knock-knock.
  Who's there?
Alison.
  Alison who?
Alison to the radio an hour or two each day.

MONEY $ RICHES

Mark Twain once said money is twice-tainted. "T'ain't yours, t'ain't mine."

* * *

Bob: "I know a place where we're sure to find lots of diamonds!"

Rob: "Let's go! Where is it?"

Bob: "In a deck of cards."

* * *

When is a library card like a credit card?
    When you use it to travel around the world.

Father: "You shouldn't waste so much money on junk toys. Don't you realize money doesn't grow on trees?"

Daughter: "Sure it does, Daddy. We always use the local bank branch, remember?"

★ ★ ★

"I know how we can save hundreds of dollars a year on long-distance phone calls," Candie told her dad.

"Wonderful," he said. "What's your plan?"

"We can call people when they're not home!"

★ ★ ★

Shelby: "My dad just threw away a $50 bill."

Wyatt: "What on earth did he do that for?"

Shelby: "It was a bill sent by a credit card company to the wrong address."

MUSIC

"Which musicians are usually the meanest?" Danielle asked.

"It's a toss-up," guessed Ellen, "between the ones who beat the drums and the ones who pick on the guitars."

✸ ✸ ✸

Which composer is squirrels' all-time favorite?

Tchaikovsky. He wrote "The Nutcracker."

✸ ✸ ✸

What kind of snake has red and yellow bands, is highly dangerous, and sings tenor?

A choral snake.

"How was the symphony concert?"

"It was wonderful! The orchestra played Vivaldi."

"Who won?"

* * *

"Can you carry a tune at all?" the grumpy talent agent asked the final try-out after a long day of auditions.

"I'll let you judge that for yourself." The auditioner confidently launched into a terrible, loud rendition of a well-known popular song.

"Well, what do you think? Can I carry a tune."

"Yes," said the agent. "Please carry it out and close the door behind you."

* * *

What do a piano and a newspaper reporter have in common?

They both make notes.

Who was the world's most famous green rock-and-roll singer?

Elvis Parsley.

* * *

"May I have the pleasure of the next dance?" Mr. Mozart asked Mrs. Mozart.

"Wait just one minuet," said Mrs. Mozart.

* * *

"Mark, I just found your guitar outside in the garbage can!" his mother said.

"I know. I put it there."

"That was your birthday present! You waited months to get it."

"Yeah, but it's no good. There's a big round hole in the middle of the sound box."

NAMES

Shelby: "Aren't you glad your mom and dad named you Lou?"

Lou: "Well, yes—but why do you ask?"

Shelby: "Because that's what all your friends call you."

* * *

What was the name of the hunter who tangled with the bear?

Claude.

* * *

What famous woman lives in New Orleans?

Louise Anna.

THE OCEAN

What happens when you tell the ocean good-bye?

It waves to you.

* * *

How do they harvest the ocean floor?

With a subtractor.

* * *

What's a sailor's favorite deli item?

A submarine sandwich.

* * *

What keeps the ocean from going dry?

Water.

Who was the greatest chef in the British Navy?
 Captain Cook.

✳ ✳ ✳

What ocean animal is the most difficult to get along with?
 The crab.

✳ ✳ ✳

Who cleans house for fish and other sea creatures?
 Mermaids.

✳ ✳ ✳

Does an octopus go around all day shaking its legs or waving its arms?

✳ ✳ ✳

What ocean always gets things absolutely right?
 The Specific Ocean.

ODDS 'n' ENDS

Who's married to Antarctica?
  Uncle Arctica.

$$* * *$$

"I can predict the future," said Carrie.
  "Sure," said Barrie. "Tell me anything at all that'll happen after today."
  "Tomorrow!" predicted Carrie.

$$* * *$$

What has four legs, seven drawers, and flies?
  Superdesk!

$$* * *$$

"Did you tell Stan the new airplane joke?"
  "Yeah, but I think it went right over his head."

What did one clock say to the other?
You tock too much.

★ ★ ★

Kristin pulled and pulled, but couldn't get the library door open.

"What's the matter?" asked a woman, approaching.

"This door must be stuck," Kristin said. "I can't pull it open."

"Can you read?" asked the woman.

"Of course I can read!" snapped Kristin.

"Then tell me what this says." The woman pointed to a word printed above the door handle. It was spelled: PUSH.

★ ★ ★

"Dad, what is cargo?"

"It's a large volume of products being moved from one place to another, usually by ship or train."

"Then why isn't it called shipgo or traingo?"

130

Mother: "Wesley, you've gotten yourself all muddy again. You just don't have much respect for your clothes and shoes, do you?"

Wesley: "I like clothes just fine, Mom. But I certainly don't think much of shoes."

Mother: "Why not?"

Wesley: "Because most of them are either loafers or sneakers."

✱ ✱ ✱

A woman stopped her car beside a child who was walking home from school. "I'm new in the neighborhood," the woman explained. "How do you get to the post office from here?"

"I ride my bicycle," answered the child.

✱ ✱ ✱

Why was the poet unable to earn a decent living?

Because rhyme does not pay.

"You're afraid to fight me!" teased Blimpo.

"No, I'm not!" shouted Shrimpy.

"Then why won't you do it?"

"Because my mother would get mad at me and spank me."

"How would your mother find out about it?"

"She'd see the ambulance taking you to the hospital."

✳ ✳ ✳

Penny: "Please open the door for me."
Annie: "It isn't a door. It's ajar."

✳ ✳ ✳

"I hear Isaac joined the army."

"Yes. He was assigned to the paratroopers. After about twelve weeks of rigorous training, he dropped out."

"That doesn't sound good."

"Yes, it was. He had to drop out of the airplane in order to complete the instruction."

132

Why did Gracie want a new fountain pen?

   The old one made a lot of mistakes.

✷ ✷ ✷

Why did the Pilgrims begin the tradition of carving turkeys on Thanksgiving?

   Because rabbits were too difficult to carve.

✷ ✷ ✷

A group of workers were building a structure above a deep old well when one of the workers lost his balance and fell into the hole. Down, down, down he went, out of sight.

   Rescue workers were summoned. They prepared ropes and lanterns, and one of them was about to descend into the dark well. "Is this well empty?" he asked the property owner.

   "It was empty until today," the owner said.

"I've discovered a foolproof cure for dan-
druff!"

"What is it?"

"Baldness."

$$\star \star \star$$

Why did the apple fall from the apple tree?

Because it was ripe.

Why did the woodpecker fall from the
apple tree?

Because its beak was stuck in the apple.

Why did the squirrel fall from the apple
tree?

Because its tail was stapled to the woodpecker.

Why did the little boy fall from the apple
tree?

He succumbed to peer pressure.

$$\star \star \star$$

Where does the Air Force store its bombs?

In Bombay.

"Charlie just got out of the hospital," said Marge.

"What was wrong with him?" asked Paul.

"He crashed his helicopter."

"How'd he do that?"

"He felt cold, so he turned the fan off."

* * *

Neighbor Gorton had a reputation for being an unpleasant old man. One day he spied a child in the branches of his largest apple tree, eating a ripe apple.

"Hey, what are you doing up there?" he demanded.

"I'm obeying your sign."

"What sign?"

"The sign that says KEEP OFF THE GRASS."

* * *

Where does a tailor buy his clothes?

Nowhere. He suits himself.

"Did you have a good time ice skating?"
Cybil's mother asked.

"Yes—until they closed the skating rink,"
Cybil said.

"Why did they close?"

"Well, it was Marvin's first time on
skates. When he stumbled into the middle
of the rink, he was so funny the ice cracked
up."

* * *

What are book covers for?
To help books get a good night's sleep.

* * *

What happens if you put too many stamps
on a letter?
It goes too far.

* * *

What comes after "o"?
Boy.

Two teenagers from a foreign country were visiting America one summer. They'd never been to a movie theater and weren't sure what to do when they arrived outside.

"You buy your tickets there at the window," explained a helpful passerby. "Then you give the tickets to the steward standing at the entrance."

The visitors dutifully bought two tickets, then walked to the entrance and handed them to the steward. The steward routinely tore them in half.

The visitors looked at each other.

"What do we do now?" asked one.

"I guess we buy two more tickets," said the other with a shrug.

✳ ✳ ✳

"What should we wear to the tea party?" asked Phyllis.

"I think we should wear our nicest tea-shirts," giggled Ginger.

Two hunters went to the Rocky Mountains to hunt mountain lions. They stopped at a trading post before entering the wilderness.

"Where can we find a good hunting guide?" they asked the trader and his customers.

"I'm the best guide around," volunteered a grizzled old trapper.

"Hogwash!" scoffed another. "You couldn't follow a railroad track."

✳ ✳ ✳

Why did the dieting man stand on the sidewalk all day long?

In an attempt to curb his appetite.

✳ ✳ ✳

"I'd like to buy a winter coat."

"How long do you need the sleeves?"

"About five months, November to March."

138

"Dad, I've decided I want to be an echo when I grow up?"

"Why do you say that?"

"If I'm an echo, I'll be able to speak every language on the planet!"

* * *

A family bought a nice lake cabin and settled in for their first weekend of peace and quiet, surrounded by the beauty of nature. Imagine their dismay to discover the faucets didn't work!

The father phoned the previous owner. "You told us there was running water!" he shouted.

"There is. Wait for the first rain, then look at the ceiling. You'll see."

* * *

"Randall broke his leg in two places!"

"What places were they? We'd better avoid them!"

How do mountains hear?
    With mountaineers.

* * *

"Don't you dare go in the dining room with dirty feet!" mom shouted. "I've just cleaned the carpet."
    "But mom, my feet are perfectly clean. That dirt you see is on my shoes."

* * *

Who steals from the rich, gives to the poor, and carries a picnic basket?
    Little Red Robin Hood.

* * *

What did one nose say to the other nose?
    "I smell something funny. Do you?"

* * *

Why do ceiling fans go around horizontally?
    Otherwise, they would be windmills.

Len: "What flying creature frequents
   schoolrooms?"
Ben: "Spelling bees?"
Len: "No. Alpha-bats."

✷ ✷ ✷

What's the difference between getting
splattered by a water balloon and getting
smeared by an egg?

   *It's the difference between getting
soaked and getting yoked.*

✷ ✷ ✷

What can run on the floor even though it
doesn't have any legs?

   Water.

✷ ✷ ✷

What did the big firecracker say to the
little firecracker?

   My pop is bigger than your pop.

PETS

A woman brought a strange-looking animal to a veterinarian's clinic. The vet did a double-take and asked, "What in the world *is* that thing?"

"It's a mattababy," the woman said.

"What's a mattababy?"

"That's what I want you to tell me."

A salesman entered a yard and saw two little girls playing with a dog.

"Does your dog bite?" he asked the children.

"Oh, no, sir. Our dog has never bitten anyone."

The salesman then walked up the steps to ring the doorbell for the parents. Suddenly, the dog jumped on the porch and bit him fiercely on the leg.

"Hey, you said your dog doesn't bite!" the salesman yelled at the girls.

"Our dog doesn't. That's somebody else's dog."

✳ ✳ ✳

The science class had show-and-tell day with pets as the theme. Mick brought in his iguana. All the children *oohed* and *ahhed* over the creature's primitive scariness.

"Why do you keep an iguana for a pet?" the teacher asked curiously.

"Because it frightens my sister," Mick replied.

"I love my pets," said Natasha. "It takes me five minutes just to say good-bye to them each morning before I come to school."

"What kind of pets do you have?" asked Mike.

"Three kittens, a hamster and two dogs."

"Well, I certainly understand. It takes me more than an hour to say good-bye to my pets every morning."

"What kind of pets do you have?"

"I have fourteen goldfish and an ant farm."

★ ★ ★

While walking his dog through the park, a man was startled by a kitten darting across the path.

"Whups, sorry!" called the kitten over its shoulder as it vanished into the shrubbery. "Please excuse me!"

The man stopped and stared, dropping his jaw. "I never knew a kitten that talked," he mumbled.

"Me, either," said the dog.

144

PLACES

What state is
always happy?
Merryland.

✳ ✳ ✳

Teacher: "Jeremy,
where can we find
the Red Sea?"
Jeremy: "Well,
there's one at the top of my last test
paper."

✳ ✳ ✳

What state can tell the most jokes?
Jokelahoma.

✳ ✳ ✳

Where do we find the Great Plains?
At the classic air museum.

"Western Canada is a fascinating place," said the teacher. "Did you know that some of the rocks you find there were deposited by glaciers?"

"But I don't see any glaciers in these pictures," said one student.

"They've gone to get more rocks," said a classmate slyly.

★ ★ ★

TONGUE TWISTER

Never freeze three breezy cheeses when sneezing.

PLANTS

What distinguishes a dogwood tree from all other trees?
   Its bark.

✱ ✱ ✱

What kind of plants do frogs enjoy most?
   Croakuses.

✱ ✱ ✱

"My grandpa likes to gather wild herbs," Myron said.
   "He must be an old-thymer," laughed Biff.

"Our mathematics teacher brought a pot plant to school and put it on her desk last week," Angie told her mother. "Today, the most amazing thing happened!"

"What was it?"

"The plant grew square roots!"

✯ ✯ ✯

What's a tree's favorite drink?

Root beer.

✯ ✯ ✯

What did the tree say to the leaf at the end of summer?

Hope you have a great fall!

✯ ✯ ✯

What are the hottest flowers in all creation?

Sunflowers.

✯ ✯ ✯

What's the tallest flower in the world?

The giraffodil.

RESTAURANTS

"Pretty short menu," said Resa, trying to decide what to order for lunch. "It's printed only on one side."

"Yeah, the other side must be for customers who are full when they arrive," said Lisa.

★ ★ ★

"I don't see spaghetti and meat sauce on this menu," complained the child.

"That's because we clean our menus after each use," said the waiter.

Brenda: "I had a dinner date at a very nice restaurant last night."
Andrea: "Who was your date?"
Brenda: "Thomas Jefferson."
Andrea: "Yeah, sure. Jefferson's been dead almost 200 years."
Brenda: "Hmmm. Now that you mention it, he didn't say much. . . ."

* * *

"Waitress, there's a fly in my soup!"

"Don't worry, sir. Nothing has ever been known to live very long in our soup."

* * *

"I have a complaint," said the diner. "Bring me your head waiter."

"He's not here," said the waiter.

"Why not? Where is he?"

"He went down the street to have a burger and some fries before the dinner crowd arrives."

Diner: "What are your breakfast specials?"
Waitress: "Today we're offering hippopota-
    mus eggs and elephant eggs."
Diner: "Give me the hippo eggs. I'm tired of
    elephant yokes."

★ ★ ★

"I'm so hungry, I could eat an elephant,"
said a customer as he sat down at a booth
in the diner.
    "Coming right up," said the waitress.

★ ★ ★

A new waitress was extremely nervous during her first evening on the job. One customer was shocked when the waitress
approached his table, clutching his rack of
lamb in both hands.
    "Please take your hands off my food!" the
diner shouted.
    "Oh, no, sir. I've already dropped it once.
I can't risk doing that again."

151

Why did the waitress lose her job?
  She refused to take orders from anyone.

* * *

Diner to Waiter: "This chicken is so tough, I'll bet Colonel Sanders killed it when he was only a buck private."

* * *

"This bread tastes funny," complained the diner.
  "But you're not laughing," commented the waiter.

* * *

"Do you want your coffee black?" asked the waitress.
  "I didn't know coffee beans grew in any other color," said the customer.

RIDDLES

What has twenty-four eyes, two tongues, two toes, and smells terrible?
A pair of used sneakers.

✳ ✳ ✳

Where can you always get satisfaction?
From the satis-FACTORY.

✳ ✳ ✳

What do lawyers wear?
Lawsuits.

✳ ✳ ✳

What kind of language do billboards use?
Sign language.

How long should a person's legs be?
   Long enough to reach the ground.

✳ ✳ ✳

What can you destroy simply by saying its name out loud?
   Silence.

✳ ✳ ✳

What has two norths, two souths, one west—but no east?
   The fifty states of the Union.

✳ ✳ ✳

What kind of fruit can you pick from a calendar?
   Dates.

✳ ✳ ✳

What do you call a cat who works for Xerox Corporation?
   A copycat.

154

Which letter of the alphabet is an island?
  T—you find it in the middle of "water."

  ✴ ✴ ✴

What has lots of teeth but never needs to see a dentist?
  A comb.

  ✴ ✴ ✴

What kind of worker gets paid to drive off her paying customers?
  The taxi driver.

  ✴ ✴ ✴

What kind of shoes are made with no leather?
  Horseshoes.

  ✴ ✴ ✴

What can travel around the world while spending its life in a corner?
  A postage stamp.

Why is the river always sleepy?
Because it has rocks in its bed.

✳ ✳ ✳

What is it that you can touch with your left foot but not your right foot?
Your right knee.

✳ ✳ ✳

What's red, has a green stem, and stays in its room most of the day?
A tomato that's been placed on probation.

✳ ✳ ✳

What kind of parties do you have in the basement?
Cellarbrations.

✳ ✳ ✳

What do a vacuum cleaner and a bookshelf have in common?
They collect dust.

What's black and white and red all over?
   A zebra with chickenpox.

★ ★ ★

What wears shoes but doesn't have feet?
   A sidewalk.

★ ★ ★

What shivers in the junkyard?
   Nervous wrecks.

★ ★ ★

What kind of tea can lighten up your home?
   Electrici-tea.

★ ★ ★

What type of can contains tons of water?
   A canal.

★ ★ ★

Who invented Kentucky-fried shoes?
   Colonel Sandals.

What two words contain more than a thousand letters?

Post office.

* * *

What's colorful, soft, has wings and is an expert in arithmetic?

A mothematician.

* * *

Do magnets get married?

No—which is remarkable, because they're all attractive.

* * *

Why do police officers need to be so strong?

So they can hold up traffic.

* * *

What are telephone calls in Persia?

Persian-to-Persian calls.

What kind of people often climb down from trees even though they never climbed up them?
   Skydivers.

★ ★ ★

What's cold and white and softly rises?
   A snowflake without a clue.

★ ★ ★

Why do firemen wear red suspenders?
   To hold their pants up.

★ ★ ★

What gets lost every time you stand up?
   Your lap.

★ ★ ★

Who makes up horror stories?
   Ghost writers.

SCHOOL

"Vocabulary test tomorrow, rain or shine," reminded the teacher as the class was dismissed.

"What if it snows?" asked Will, hopefully.

* * *

"How many letters are in the alphabet?" the teacher asked.

"Twenty-one," said Edward.

"No! You know there are twenty-six."

"Not right now. The D.A. and the F.B.I. are in federal court."

160

Teacher: "Resa, name five animals you might find in Africa."

Resa: "A lion, an elephant. . .and three zebras."

✳ ✳ ✳

"Trina, you seem to be having a lot of trouble with your spelling assignments," the teacher said.

"Yes. I guess words intimidate me."

"But they're only words! Words can't hurt you."

"I suppose not—unless you get hit by a dictionary."

✳ ✳ ✳

"Gayle, your handwriting is terrible," her father said.

"Yes, I know. I scribble deliberately."

"Why don't you want to write clearly?"

"This way, it's harder for the teacher to catch all my misspellings."

"What did you score on those two exams today?" Gina's mother asked as Gina wearily flung her backpack on the dining table.

"A hundred," Gina replied.

"That's wonderful! You've never made an A in history before!"

"Well, actually, I scored 50 in history and 50 in math."

★ ★ ★

Linda: "The teacher caught Winkie cheating on his reading test."

Rob: "Winkie knows cheating is dishonest. That was silly."

Linda: "Yeah—and even worse than you think."

Rob: "What do you mean?"

Linda: "The way the teacher knew he had cheated was his answer to the fourth question. The student sitting in front of him wrote, 'I don't know the answer.' Winkie wrote, 'I don't know the answer, either.'"

"Mindy, why are your grades so low on this report card?" mother asked.

"Oh, it's that time of year," Mindy said. "You know everything is marked down after the holiday season."

∗ ∗ ∗

Teacher: "Can you name something that's harder than a diamond?"
Student: "Yes—paying for one."

∗ ∗ ∗

Two children met for the first time while walking home at the end of the first day of school.

"What's your name?" asked one.

"Jim White. What's yours?"

"Pete."

"Got a last name?"

"Well, I used to think my name was Pete Jenkins. But after today, I think it's Pete Be-quiet."

"I have good news and bad news," said the teacher. "The good news is that we're having only half a day of school this morning."

The class went wild with joy until the teacher quieted them.

"The bad news," he said, "is that we'll have the other half this afternoon."

★ ★ ★

"Where do we get pineapples?" asked the teacher.

"From pine trees," guessed the student.

★ ★ ★

Teacher: "Shirley, compose a sentence that begins with 'I.'"

Shirley: "I is—"

Teacher: "Never say, 'I is.' It's 'He is' or 'She is,' but 'I am.' Begin your sentence, 'I am. . . .'"

Shirley: "I am the ninth letter of the alphabet."

164

"Did you play hooky from school yesterday to go fishing?" the teacher asked.

"No, sir," said Dennis. "I played hooky to go to the carnival."

✳ ✳ ✳

"I didn't see you in any of our classes yesterday," said Kimberly. "You must've missed school."

"Not much," said Kenneth.

✳ ✳ ✳

"What is a synonym?" the English teacher asked.

"It's one of the words I use when I can't spell the main word," the honest student replied.

✳ ✳ ✳

Teacher: "Who's the Speaker of the House?"
Student: "Daddy."

"Did you learn anything at school today?" Jeff's dad asked.

"I guess not," Jeff said. "They're making us return tomorrow."

★ ★ ★

Teacher: "What's the difference between elephants in Africa and elephants in India?"
Vinnie: "A couple thousand miles."

★ ★ ★

Why was Mrs. Johnson's class abuzz?
It was having a spelling bee.

★ ★ ★

Mother was reading in the den when Beth came to the door. "Mom, do you think you could sign your name in the dark?"

"I've never tried, dear, but I probably could."

"Good!" said Beth, switching off the light. "I need for you to sign my report card."

Teacher: "Jamie, how do you spell 'canoe'?"
Jamie: "K-n-e-w."

★ ★ ★

A rule was posted in large letters in the school hallway: SHOES REQUIRED IN THE CAFETERIA.

In the margin, someone had scribbled: SOCKS MUST GO TO THE GYM.

★ ★ ★

Mother was eager to hear about Brenda's first day at school. "So how do you think you're doing so far?"

"Well, apparently, I'm one of the advanced students," Brenda remarked.

"Oh, really? What makes you think that?"

"They put me at the head of a row."

★ ★ ★

What kind of notebook grows near trees?
Loose leaf.

SCIENCE

What kind of chewing gum do scientists prefer?

Experiment Gum.

* * *

"Do you know why lightning rarely strikes the same place twice?" asked the science teacher.

"Because after lightning strikes it the first time," a bright student responded, "the same place is *gone!*"

Teacher: "Who was the first person to circle the earth in space?"
Student: "The man in the moon."

* * *

"What would happen if there was no such thing as gravity?" the teacher asked.
"We could all fly!" came the answer.

* * *

"The spaceships of the next century will travel faster than the speed of light!" the science teacher marveled to her class.
"Then what kind of lights will they have inside them?" asked a student.

* * *

"Do you understand exactly what biology is?" the teacher asked on the first day of class.
One student raised her hand. "I think it's the science my mom practices whenever she goes to the shopping mall."

What do astronomers do to relax?
  They enjoy reading comet books.

* * *

Science Teacher: "How can herpetologists tell the age of a snake?"
Student: "Track down its birth certificate."

* * *

What did the seismologist say to the earthquake?
  "This is all your fault."

* * *

"I think Thomas Edison must have been the most brilliant person who ever lived," said Kate.

  "What makes you think so?" asked her teacher.

  "He invented the light bulb. Then, to give people a reason to keep the lights on all night, he invented the phonograph!"

170

What was Voltaire famous for?
He invented the volt.

★ ★ ★

What kind of telephones do they use in the space shuttle?
Phones with very long cords.

★ ★ ★

Why did Benjamin Franklin make the first eyeglasses?
To make a spectacle of himself.

★ ★ ★

What goes up when you count down?
A rocket.

SPORTS

When is a football team like an airplane?
When it makes a touchdown.

* * *

An auctioneer was persuaded to join some friends in a round of golf. He'd never been on a golf course before.

"Fore!" shouted one of his friends, hitting a tee shot.

"Do I hear four and a quarter?" barked the auctioneer without thinking.

Two boys attended a high school basketball game.

"Boy, that big forward for the other team sure is tall!" marveled one.

"Yeah, I'll bet he needs a ladder to shave," said the other.

✶ ✶ ✶

What does a cake have in common with a baseball game?
The batter.

✶ ✶ ✶

What's purple and has twenty-two legs, four backs and two ends?
A football team from Mars.

✶ ✶ ✶

Mother: "Did you hear that shattering noise? It sounded like a window breaking."
Son: "Didn't hear a thing, Mom. Have you seen our softball?"

A baseball pitcher was so angry he screamed at the first baseman, screamed at the shortstop, and screamed at the catcher. Finally, he took off his glove, slung it on the mound and began stomping on it, still screaming.

"What in the world does he think he's doing?" one outfielder called to another.

"He's throwing his best pitch, known as a tantrum."

★ ★ ★

"Dad! Dad! I won the gold medal in the broad jump!"

"That's terrific! I know you're proud."

"Yeah. May I have $20?"

"What for?"

"To have it bronzed."

★ ★ ★

What sport do mosquitoes enjoy?
   Skindiving.

174

"Hey, I've got great news for you!" Brewster said to his buddy Val after the track and field tryouts. "I just overheard the coaches say they've selected you for the hammer throw unit."

"That's great!" Val yelled. "I'd better start practicing, huh?"

"Well, actually," said Brewster, his smile disappearing, "there's sort of a down side to it."

"What do you mean?"

"They want you to be the catcher."

★ ★ ★

What does a football game have in common with a dollar?

It consists of four quarters.

★ ★ ★

What happens when two ropes get into a contest?

They always tie.

What do skydivers do when their parachutes don't open?

They yell for the airplane crew to lower a rope.

★ ★ ★

Why do runners stretch their legs before beginning a race?

They know if they can make their legs longer, they'll run faster!

★ ★ ★

What's black and white and goes 150 miles an hour?

A newspaper being read by a stockcar driver.

★ ★ ★

Why did the basketball team flood the gymnasium?

It was the only way they could sink any baskets.

"I keep my baseball glove in the car," said Bruce, making a detour to fetch it before joining the neighborhood ball game.

"Why do you keep it there?" asked Vernon.

"The car has a glove compartment."

★ ★ ★

Why did the golfer carry an extra shirt and pair of pants in his golf bag?

In case he got a hole in one.

★ ★ ★

Which Olympic athletes operate moving van lines in their later years?

The boxers.

★ ★ ★

What do baseball players on third base like to sing?

"There's no place like home."

TALL TALES

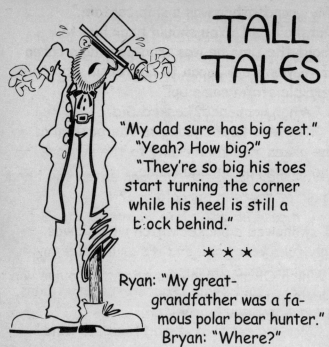

"My dad sure has big feet."
"Yeah? How big?"
"They're so big his toes start turning the corner while his heel is still a block behind."

* * *

Ryan: "My great-grandfather was a famous polar bear hunter."
Bryan: "Where?"
Ryan: "In Mississippi."
Bryan: "No way! There are no polar bears in Mississippi."
Ryan: "Nope, not since my great-grandfather finished with 'em."

178

"My grandfather was a ship captain," Marshall said. "You should hear him tell about the time he was transporting a cargo of yo-yos from Japan to California, and this terrible storm came up!"

"What happened?" asked Sid.

"The ship kept sinking to the bottom of the ocean, and then rising to the surface, and sinking again, and rising. . . ."

★ ★ ★

"I swallowed a pocket watch when I was only four years old, and it's still inside my stomach," said Jacque.

"Wow!" said Jean. "That's gruesome! Does it ever give you a problem?"

"No—except that it's difficult to wind."

★ ★ ★

They say Abraham Lincoln was so tall it took his head five minutes to realize his toes were frozen.

"I've figured out how to catch man-eating tigers," announced Gilbert.

"Oh, really?" his father said. "What tools would you use?"

"Binoculars, tweezers and a paper sack," Gilbert said confidently.

"This sounds fascinating. What's your method?"

"I hide in a tree until I see a man-eating tiger coming, way off in the distance. I turn the binoculars backward and look at the tiger through the wrong end. This shrinks the tiger to the size of a fly. Then I just grab the little critter with the tweezers and whisk it into the bag."

★ ★ ★

Brittany: "My great-grandfather helped build the Grand Coulee Dam."
Artie: "That's nothing. My great-grandfather helped kill the Dead Sea."

VACATION

"Ma'am, I need to buy a nonstop plane ticket to New York City, please," the Montana rancher told the airline agent.

The agent checked the flight schedule. "We can't get you to New York nonstop from here. We can get you there via Buffalo."

The rancher thought it over. "Well," he said, "I've never ridden a buffalo, but I'll give it a try."

★ ★ ★

Where do dogs love to go on vacation?
  To Jellystone Bark.

Two children played the age-old game of counting cows while riding in the back seat of their parents' car.

"I just spotted one!" shouted one child.

"Don't be ridiculous," scoffed the other. "That cow already had spots."

✱ ✱ ✱

"I thought you complained that it rained the whole time you were on vacation," Matt said. "So how did you get such a great suntan?"

"This is not a suntan," said Pat. "This is a rusty body."

✱ ✱ ✱

TONGUE TWISTER

Meek Nick eats green grapes.
Bleak Mick meets Greek apes.

WEATHER

"Did you hear they've scheduled the town Christmas parade Saturday afternoon?"

"Yes. I wonder what will happen if it snows Saturday afternoon?"

"Then I guess they'll have to hold the parade Saturday morning."

* * *

What hold up the sun?
Sunbeams.

* * *

How do people who live in the desert stay cool?
They take turns standing in one another's shadow.

"What's the difference between weather and climate?" the teacher asked.

"Weather is the abbreviation for climate," one student volunteered.

★ ★ ★

"We sure have been getting a lot of rain," Andrew commented.

"Yeah," agreed Tonya. "I hope they've started building an ark down at the zoo."

★ ★ ★

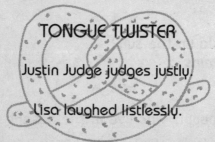

TONGUE TWISTER

Justin Judge judges justly.

Lisa laughed listlessly.

WHAT DO YOU GET WHEN. . . ?

. . .you cross a school bus with an octopus?
An octo bus.

★ ★ ★

. . .you cross a parrot with a monkey?
A critter that can explain all the mischief it gets into.

★ ★ ★

. . .you take a dog to a beauty parlor?
A shampoodle.

★ ★ ★

. . .you cross a hunting dog with a gold football uniform?
A golden receiver.

. . .you cross a lion with a computer?
A maneframe.

★ ★ ★

. . .you cross mathematics with seaweed?
Algae-bra.

★ ★ ★

. . .you cross a crab and a mockingbird?
A walkie-talkie.

★ ★ ★

. . .you put a rotor blade on a snail?
A shellicopter.

★ ★ ★

. . .you cross a hog with a tree?
Porky Twig.

★ ★ ★

. . .you cross an octopus with a chicken?
Lots of drumsticks.

. . .you cross a mathematical genius with a basketball star?

A fine mathlete.

* * *

. . .you cross a groundhog with a basketball net?

An extended basketball season.

* * *

. . .you start across a river in a rotten boat?

No further than half way.

* * *

. . .you cross a kangaroo with a cement truck?

Potholes across the Outback.

* * *

. . .you cross a skunk with a rattlesnake?

Something you wouldn't want to share a locker with.

. . .you cross a church steeple with a pair of jeans?

Bellbottoms.

* * *

. . .you assign Superman to a computer crash?

A screensaver.

* * *

. . .you cross a church bell with a humming-bird?

A humdinger.

* * *

. . .you cross an orange with a famous story-teller?

Mother Juice.

* * *

. . .your cat swallows a ball of yarn?

Mittens!

. . .you cross a concrete truck with a chicken?
  A block layer.

★ ★ ★

. . .you put a cow on a trampoline?
  A gigantic milkshake.

★ ★ ★

. . .you cross an octopus with a cow?
  A cow that can draw its own milk.

★ ★ ★

. . .you cross a cow with a chicken?
  Roost beef.

★ ★ ★

. . .you cross a snowman with a guard dog?
  Frostbite.

★ ★ ★

. . .you cross a bulldog with a computer?
  Both a bark and a byte.

. . .you cross a skunk with a honey-colored bear?
Winnie the Pe-yew!

* * *

. . .a reptile scientist marries a funeral home director?
Hiss and hearse.

* * *

. . .you cross a dentist with a wild animal?
A molar bear.

* * *

TONGUE TWISTER

Three blind mice blew bugles.

Floyd fed the flies fried fly food.

Sue Sleuth slowly solved the sloppy case.

WORK & PLAY

"You children watch too much TV and sit around and do nothing all day," Father scolded. "You should come help me work in the yard."

"But it's too much trouble," protested Jessica.

"Nonsense. Work is good for you."

"Then shouldn't we save some for tomorrow?"

AWESOME BOOKS FOR KIDS!

The Young Reader's Christian Library
Action, Adventure, and Fun Reading!

This series for young readers ages 8 to 12 is action-packed, fast-paced, and Christ-centered! With exciting illustrations on every other page following the text, kids won't be able to put these books down! Over 100 illustrations per book. All books are paperbound. The unique size (4 ⅛" x 5 ⅜") makes these books easy to take anywhere!

A Great Selection to Satisfy All Kids!

Abraham Lincoln	Elijah	Miriam
Billy Graham	Esther	Moses
Billy Sunday	Florence	Paul
Christopher	Nightingale	Peter
Columbus	Hudson Taylor	The Pilgrim's
Clara Barton	In His Steps	Progress
Corrie ten Boom	Jesus	Roger Williams
Daniel	Jim Elliot	Ruth
David	Joseph	Samuel
David Brainerd	Little Women	Samuel Morris
David Livingstone	Luis Palau	Sojourner Truth
Deborah	Lydia	

Available wherever books are sold.
Or order from: Barbour Publishing, Inc., P.O. Box 719
Uhrichsville, Ohio 44683
http://www.barbourbooks.com

$2.50 each retail, plus $1.00 for postage and handling per order.
Prices subject to change without notice.